Kalkiism Is Not Communism

Paramendra Kumar Bhagat

Book Outline: *Kalkiism Is Not Communism*

Introduction: (Page 6)

- Introduce the concept of Kalkiism and its distinction from capitalism and communism.
- Set the stage for the need for a new system, emphasizing the flaws of GDP-based economies and the societal inequalities under current systems.

Chapter 1: The Birth of Kalkiism (Page 9)

- Historical background and philosophical underpinnings of Kalkiism.
- Introduce the concept of Gross Domestic Requirement (GDR) and its contrast with Gross Domestic Product (GDP).
- Describe the vision of a time-based economy.

Chapter 2: Time as the New Currency (Page 14)

- Explain how the time unit works as the universal currency.
- Discuss how wages are standardized across all professions, creating a level playing field.
- Examples of how transactions would work in this economy (e.g., purchasing goods, services, or experiences).

Chapter 3: Redefining Work and Value (Page 20)

- Explore the inclusivity of work, acknowledging contributions like household management and caregiving.
- Discuss the social and psychological impacts of equal hourly wages across professions.

- Highlight case studies or hypothetical scenarios to illustrate fairness and productivity.

Chapter 4: Building the Kalkiist Market (Page 26)

- The role of vibrant markets in a time-based economy.
- How supply and demand function without traditional currency.
- Mechanisms for ensuring abundance and avoiding scarcity.

Chapter 5: Democracy Redefined (Page 32)

- Kalkiism as a driver of true democracy, eliminating economic hierarchies.
- Explore how economic equality enhances political and social equity.
- Mechanisms to prevent corruption and ensure transparency.

Chapter 6: Innovation and the Cambrian Explosion of Productivity (Page 38)

- How Kalkiism encourages unprecedented human cooperation.
- Discuss examples of potential breakthroughs in technology, art, and science.
- The interplay of freedom and equality in fostering innovation.

Chapter 7: Eliminating Poverty and Scarcity (Page 45)

- Detailed exploration of how Kalkiism eradicates poverty and raises living standards universally.

- Address potential challenges and solutions in implementing GDR at a global scale.
- Compare Kalkiism's approach to poverty reduction with that of communism and capitalism.

Chapter 8: A Day in the Life of a Kalkiist Society (Page 52)

- Paint a vivid picture of everyday life under Kalkiism.
- Highlight the simplicity of transactions, the vibrancy of the market, and the harmony of society.
- Describe personal stories of individuals thriving in this new system.

Chapter 9: Myths and Misconceptions (Page 57)

- Address common critiques and misunderstandings about Kalkiism.
- Clarify why Kalkiism is not communism or capitalism and how it avoids the pitfalls of both.
- Discuss the transition process and potential roadblocks.

Chapter 10: A New World Order (Page 64)

- Envision the global implications of Kalkiism.
- Discuss the potential for international cooperation and the dissolution of economic disparities between nations.
- Conclude with an inspiring call to action, inviting readers to imagine and work toward this revolutionary future.

Conclusion: (Page 70)

- Reflect on the transformative power of new economic paradigms.

- Reaffirm the core message: Kalkiism is not communism, but a fundamentally new and promising approach to equality and prosperity.

Epilogue: From Theory to Practice – The Path to Implementing Kalkiism in Nepal (Page 72)

Kalkiism: A Revolutionary Alternative to Capitalism and Communism

The 21st century finds humanity at a crossroads, with capitalism and communism dominating the economic discourse. Both systems, though vastly different, have failed to address the fundamental issues of inequality, poverty, and environmental sustainability. Enter Kalkiism, a visionary new economic framework that seeks to transcend the limitations of these traditional paradigms. By replacing Gross Domestic Product (GDP) with Gross Domestic Requirement (GDR) and introducing a time-based economy, Kalkiism redefines value, equity, and productivity. It is neither capitalism nor communism, but a revolutionary alternative that promises prosperity for all.

At the heart of Kalkiism lies a profound shift in how we measure economic success. GDP, the cornerstone of capitalist economies, focuses on the total market value of goods and services produced. However, GDP fails to account for wealth distribution, environmental degradation, and unpaid but essential work, such as caregiving and household management. Capitalism's emphasis on competition and profit often leads to significant wealth disparities, leaving millions in poverty while a small elite accumulates immense wealth. Meanwhile, communism, which aimed to eliminate these inequalities, historically delivered scarcity, inefficiency, and authoritarianism. Both systems have perpetuated cycles of inequity and dissatisfaction, leaving a gap for a new approach.

Kalkiism fills this void by introducing Gross Domestic Requirement (GDR), a metric designed to align economic output with the actual needs of society. Unlike GDP, which measures production for profit, GDR focuses on ensuring every individual has access to the essentials of life: food, shelter, education, healthcare, and more. This shift in focus transforms the economy from one that prioritizes accumulation to one that prioritizes sufficiency and well-being.

Central to Kalkiism's vision is its time-based economy, where the universal currency is time itself. Under this system, every individual earns an hourly wage—whether they are a farmer, doctor, artist, or president. There is no money, no cash; only time.

If you work eight hours, you earn eight hours. Goods and services are priced in seconds, minutes, or hours, ensuring fair exchange and eliminating the exploitative nature of traditional monetary systems. This framework values all forms of labor equally, recognizing the contributions of everyone, including women and caregivers, who are often undervalued or unpaid in GDP-driven economies.

Kalkiism also envisions vibrant, dynamic markets, challenging the misconception that it mirrors communism's centralized control. Unlike communism, Kalkiism encourages innovation and productivity by fostering unprecedented human cooperation. With every individual's basic needs met, creativity and entrepreneurship flourish, unleashing a "Cambrian explosion" of ideas and solutions. This leads to abundance, not scarcity, and ensures a high standard of living for all—not just for a privileged few.

In summary, Kalkiism is neither capitalism nor communism. It is a fundamentally new paradigm that seeks to eliminate poverty, inequality, and inefficiency while fostering democracy, innovation, and cooperation. By redefining value through GDR and a time-based currency, Kalkiism offers humanity the chance to build a fairer, more prosperous world. The flaws of our current systems demand bold solutions, and Kalkiism stands ready to lead the way.

Chapter 1: The Birth of Kalkiism: A Philosophical and Economic Revolution

The modern world, characterized by globalization, technological advancements, and unprecedented wealth creation, is also plagued by stark inequality, poverty, and environmental degradation. Both capitalism and communism, the dominant economic systems of the last two centuries, have failed to create a sustainable and equitable society. Capitalism's focus on profit maximization has led to extreme wealth concentration and exploitation, while communism's promise of equality often devolved into authoritarianism and inefficiency. It is within this context that Kalkiism emerges—a transformative economic and philosophical framework aimed at addressing the flaws of its predecessors and paving the way for a fairer and more sustainable world.

Historical Roots and Philosophical Underpinnings

Kalkiism derives its name and inspiration from the figure of Kalki in Hindu mythology, often seen as a harbinger of change and renewal. This symbolism is apt, as Kalkiism seeks to usher in a new era of economic justice and human cooperation. The framework takes a human-centric approach, viewing economic systems as tools to enhance well-being rather than mechanisms for unchecked growth or rigid control. Kalkiism acknowledges the lessons of history: the social stratification and environmental degradation perpetuated by capitalism and the economic stagnation and loss of freedom under communism. By addressing these historical failures, Kalkiism positions itself as a philosophy of renewal, blending innovation with equity.

Philosophically, Kalkiism rests on three core tenets:

1. **Universal Equity**: Every individual, regardless of occupation, is of equal intrinsic value and should have equal access to society's resources.

2. **Sufficiency Over Accumulation**: The goal of an economy is to meet the needs of all rather than to perpetuate limitless growth.
3. **Cooperation Over Competition**: Human progress is best achieved through collective effort rather than cutthroat competition.

These principles form the foundation of Kalkiism and guide its revolutionary approach to measuring and managing economic activity.

From GDP to GDR: Redefining Economic Metrics

One of Kalkiism's most significant innovations is the replacement of Gross Domestic Product (GDP) with Gross Domestic Requirement (GDR). GDP, the traditional measure of economic success, calculates the total monetary value of goods and services produced within a country. While widely used, GDP is fundamentally flawed as a metric for societal well-being. It prioritizes economic growth without considering the distribution of wealth, environmental costs, or the value of unpaid labor such as caregiving and community service. Under GDP, activities that harm society—such as pollution or deforestation—can perversely contribute to economic "growth" because they generate financial transactions.

In contrast, GDR measures the total resources and services required to meet the basic needs of a population. These needs include food, shelter, healthcare, education, and access to cultural and recreational opportunities. By focusing on what is required for a society to thrive rather than what can be produced for profit, GDR shifts the emphasis from accumulation to sufficiency. It acknowledges that an economy's primary goal should be to ensure the well-being of its people, not to generate wealth for a select few. This paradigm shift challenges deeply entrenched notions of success and demands a reevaluation of what constitutes progress.

Under the GDR framework, economic activity is directed toward meeting these defined needs. Once the requirements of a population are met, additional production and innovation are encouraged but not at the expense of social equity or environmental sustainability. This focus on necessity over excess reduces waste, ensures a fair distribution of resources, and fosters a sense of shared purpose.

The Vision of a Time-Based Economy

Perhaps the most radical aspect of Kalkiism is its reimagining of currency. In a Kalkiist society, money is replaced with time as the universal medium of exchange. This time-based economy operates on the principle that all labor, regardless of its nature, is of equal value because it represents the same finite resource: human time. Whether an individual is a farmer, teacher, doctor, or artist, they earn the same hourly wage, measured in time units.

For example, an eight-hour workday earns eight hours of credit. Goods and services are priced in seconds, minutes, or hours, reflecting the time invested in their production or provision. A loaf of bread might cost ten minutes, while a medical consultation might cost one hour. This system eliminates the disparities in income and purchasing power that plague capitalist economies, where some individuals earn in minutes what others earn in months.

A time-based economy also redefines the concept of work. Activities traditionally excluded from economic valuation, such as caregiving, household management, and community volunteering, are fully recognized and compensated. This inclusivity not only addresses gender disparities but also fosters a sense of dignity and value in all forms of labor.

Practical Implications of a Time-Based Economy

The transition to a time-based economy involves significant structural changes but offers profound benefits:

1. **Equality of Opportunity**: By standardizing wages, Kalkiism ensures that everyone has the same earning potential, regardless of profession or background.
2. **Elimination of Poverty**: With GDR as the guiding metric, basic needs are universally met, effectively eradicating poverty.

3. **Reduction of Greed and Corruption**: The absence of monetary wealth diminishes the incentive for exploitation and corruption.
4. **Enhanced Cooperation**: With no competition for excessive wealth, individuals and organizations are motivated to collaborate for the common good.

The system also accommodates vibrant markets, contrary to the misconception that Kalkiism resembles communism's centralized planning. Markets in a time-based economy are dynamic and diverse, offering a wide range of goods and services priced in time. Consumers have choice and autonomy, while producers and innovators are rewarded with time credits, encouraging creativity and entrepreneurship.

Addressing Potential Criticisms

Critics may argue that a time-based economy undervalues specialized skills or fails to incentivize innovation. However, Kalkiism addresses these concerns by recognizing that innovation and expertise are driven by intrinsic motivations, such as curiosity, passion, and the desire to contribute, rather than purely financial rewards. Moreover, the universal recognition of all labor fosters a culture of respect and mutual support, creating an environment where everyone can excel.

Another challenge is the practical implementation of a time-based system in a world accustomed to money. Kalkiism proposes gradual transitions, starting with pilot programs in local communities and expanding as the model proves its efficacy. Advances in digital technology, such as blockchain and time-tracking applications, make the logistical aspects of a time-based economy increasingly feasible.

A New Dawn for Humanity

Kalkiism is not merely an economic system; it is a call to reimagine human society. By replacing GDP with GDR and introducing a time-based currency, Kalkiism shifts the focus from profit to people, from competition to cooperation, and from scarcity to abundance. It represents a bold vision of a world where everyone's needs are met, and everyone's contributions are valued equally.

The birth of Kalkiism marks the beginning of a new chapter in humanity's journey—a chapter defined not by the accumulation of wealth but by the pursuit of shared prosperity and dignity for all. As we confront the challenges of inequality, environmental crises, and social fragmentation, Kalkiism offers a beacon of hope, inviting us to build a world that reflects our highest ideals.

Chapter 2: Time as the New Currency

In the age of capitalist and monetary economies, currency has served as a fundamental mechanism for facilitating trade, assigning value, and accumulating wealth. However, traditional currency systems are deeply flawed. They perpetuate inequality, favoring those who inherit or acquire wealth, while marginalizing those without access to financial capital. Under capitalism, money creates hierarchies, distorting the value of labor and prioritizing profit over fairness. Time-based economies, the cornerstone of Kalkiism, aim to resolve these inequities by redefining the concept of value and currency itself. By replacing money with time as the universal currency, Kalkiism establishes an egalitarian foundation where all labor is valued equally, ensuring fairness and promoting social harmony.

Time as the Universal Currency

In a Kalkiist economy, time becomes the sole unit of exchange. The logic is simple yet profound: time is the one resource that is equally available to every human being. Regardless of background, talent, or circumstance, every individual possesses the same 24 hours in a day. By tying currency to time, Kalkiism ensures that all contributions to society, whether manual, intellectual, or creative, are valued equally.

Under this system, individuals earn time units for their labor. For every hour worked, an individual earns one hour in currency. These time units can then be used to purchase goods and services, which are priced in terms of the time required to produce or provide them. This simple yet revolutionary approach eliminates income disparities and creates a truly equitable economic framework.

Standardized Wages Across Professions

One of the most striking features of a time-based economy is the standardization of wages. In the current capitalist system, wages vary drastically based on the perceived value of a profession, often leading to significant income inequality. For instance, a corporate executive might earn in an hour what a manual laborer earns in a month. These discrepancies are not only unjust but also fail to acknowledge the intrinsic value of all forms of work.

Kalkiism challenges this notion by asserting that all labor is equally valuable because it requires the same finite resource: time. Whether one is a doctor, teacher, farmer, or artist, the hourly wage remains the same. This system recognizes that every role contributes to the functioning and well-being of society. A farmer who grows food, a teacher who educates the next generation, and a doctor who saves lives are all essential, and their time is equally precious.

By standardizing wages, Kalkiism levels the economic playing field. It eliminates the exploitation of workers and ensures that everyone, regardless of their profession, has equal earning potential. This not only fosters social cohesion but also encourages individuals to pursue careers based on passion and aptitude rather than financial incentives.

Transactions in a Time-Based Economy

The mechanics of a time-based economy are straightforward yet transformative. Goods and services are priced based on the time required to produce or deliver them. This pricing model reflects the true value of labor and resources, free from the distortions of monetary profit margins. Below are examples of how transactions would work in a Kalkiist economy:

Buying a Loaf of Bread

Imagine a farmer spends an hour growing wheat, a miller spends 30 minutes grinding it into flour, and a baker spends another hour baking the bread. The total cost of a loaf of bread would then be two and a half hours, distributed among the contributors. A consumer purchases the bread by deducting 2 hours and 30 minutes from their time credit balance.

Accessing Healthcare

In a time-based economy, a medical consultation might be priced at one hour, reflecting the time the doctor dedicates to the appointment. The cost is the same whether the patient is a wealthy executive or a manual laborer, ensuring equal access to healthcare services.

Education as a Right

In a Kalkiist society, education is valued as a societal investment rather than a commercial transaction. A teacher earns time credits for the hours they spend educating students, but the students themselves do not "pay" for education. Instead, society collectively allocates time resources to ensure universal access to knowledge and skill development.

Entertainment and Leisure

An artist might charge two hours for creating a painting, while a movie ticket might cost one hour per person. These transactions not only sustain creators but also make cultural experiences accessible to all, regardless of their social or economic status.

Practical Benefits of Time-Based Transactions

1. Economic Equality

By removing monetary wealth from the equation, Kalkiism ensures that no individual or group wields disproportionate power over others. Equal wages mean equal purchasing power, fostering a more harmonious and inclusive society.

2. Transparency

Time-based pricing is inherently transparent. Consumers know exactly how much labor went into a product or service, promoting fairness and reducing exploitation.

3. Encouragement of Cooperation

A time-based economy encourages collaboration over competition. Businesses and individuals are incentivized to work together to optimize processes and reduce the time required for production, benefiting both producers and consumers.

4. Recognition of All Work

Activities traditionally excluded from economic valuation, such as caregiving, community service, and household management, are fully integrated into the Kalkiist economy. A parent caring for their child earns the same time credits as a scientist conducting groundbreaking research, ensuring that all forms of labor are valued.

Addressing Potential Criticisms

Critics of a time-based economy may raise concerns about the valuation of specialized skills or the potential lack of incentives for innovation. Kalkiism addresses these issues by emphasizing that intrinsic motivation, such as curiosity, creativity, and the desire to contribute, often drives human innovation more effectively than financial incentives. For example, many of history's greatest inventors and thinkers pursued their work out of passion rather than monetary gain.

Additionally, while all labor is valued equally in terms of time, the system still allows for specialization and expertise. A surgeon, for instance, would still need extensive training and skill development, but their time in surgery is valued equally to the time a farmer spends growing crops. This approach fosters respect for all professions and eliminates the hierarchy that currently divides society.

The Role of Technology

Advances in digital technology make the practical implementation of a time-based economy increasingly feasible. Blockchain technology, for instance, could be used to track and verify time credits, ensuring transparency and preventing fraud. Mobile applications could facilitate transactions, making it easy for individuals to earn, save, and spend their time units.

Technology also enables efficient record-keeping and resource allocation, ensuring that society's needs are met without unnecessary bureaucracy. By leveraging these tools, Kalkiism can create a seamless and user-friendly economic system that benefits everyone.

Transforming Society

A time-based economy represents more than just a shift in currency; it is a reimagining of societal values. By prioritizing fairness, equality, and cooperation, Kalkiism creates a framework where individuals are empowered to contribute meaningfully to society without fear of exploitation or poverty. The elimination of income disparity fosters social cohesion, while the universal recognition of all labor promotes dignity and respect.

The adoption of time as the universal currency has the potential to transform not only economic systems but also human relationships. It encourages empathy, understanding, and shared purpose, laying the foundation for a more equitable and harmonious world.

Conclusion

Time is the most universal and egalitarian resource available to humanity. By adopting a time-based economy, Kalkiism offers a bold and innovative solution to the flaws of monetary systems, creating a society where all labor is valued equally and everyone has equal access to resources. Transactions become simple, transparent, and fair, ensuring that no one is left behind. In doing so, Kalkiism not only redefines currency but also reimagines what it means to live in a just and equitable society.

Chapter 3: Redefining Work and Value

For centuries, the concept of work has been narrowly defined and deeply influenced by societal hierarchies and economic systems. In traditional capitalist economies, work is often equated with employment that generates monetary profit, while other vital contributions, such as caregiving, household management, and community service, are marginalized or ignored altogether. This approach not only perpetuates inequality but also undervalues essential roles that sustain the social fabric. Kalkiism, with its emphasis on equality and inclusivity, redefines work and value by recognizing all contributions to society as equally important. Through its innovative framework of equal hourly wages, Kalkiism fosters fairness, dignity, and productivity, challenging outdated notions of worth.

The Inclusivity of Work

One of Kalkiism's most transformative principles is the recognition of all forms of labor, regardless of whether they occur in the formal economy or within households and communities. Traditional economic systems often fail to value unpaid work, such as raising children, caring for elderly family members, or maintaining a home. This neglect disproportionately affects women, who historically bear the brunt of unpaid domestic responsibilities.

Kalkiism addresses this inequity by acknowledging that all labor requires time and effort and contributes to societal well-being. Whether an individual is cultivating crops, performing surgery, or caring for a sick relative, their work is equally valued under the Kalkiist framework. By compensating all contributions with equal hourly wages, Kalkiism ensures that no one's efforts are overlooked or devalued.

Household Management and Caregiving

In a Kalkiist society, household management and caregiving are treated as legitimate professions. A parent who spends eight hours caring for their child earns the same amount of time credits as a scientist conducting research or an engineer designing infrastructure. This inclusivity not only provides financial security for caregivers but also elevates the social status of these roles, recognizing their vital contribution to society.

For example, consider a single mother who dedicates her time to raising two children. In a traditional economy, her labor would go unrecognized, leaving her financially dependent or struggling to balance unpaid caregiving with paid employment. In a Kalkiist economy, her work is fully compensated, ensuring her financial independence and reinforcing the value of her contribution.

The Social and Psychological Impacts of Equal Hourly Wages

The concept of equal hourly wages is revolutionary in its potential to reshape societal attitudes toward work and value. By standardizing wages across all professions, Kalkiism challenges deeply ingrained hierarchies that prioritize certain types of labor over others.

Promoting Equality and Reducing Social Hierarchies

Under the current system, occupations such as investment banking or corporate leadership are often rewarded disproportionately, while essential roles like teaching, farming, or sanitation work are undervalued. This creates a skewed perception of worth, where individuals are judged by their income rather than their contributions to society.

In contrast, Kalkiism's equal hourly wage system promotes a culture of equality. A teacher's time is as valuable as a CEO's, and a janitor's efforts are as respected as those of a software engineer. This revaluation fosters mutual respect among professions and reduces the stigma associated with traditionally undervalued roles.

Alleviating Stress and Anxiety

The financial pressures of modern economies contribute to widespread stress, anxiety, and burnout. The fear of unemployment, the struggle to make ends meet, and the constant pursuit of higher earnings take a toll on mental health. In a Kalkiist economy, where wages are standardized and basic needs are universally met, these anxieties are alleviated.

Individuals are free to pursue careers aligned with their passions and talents, knowing that their work will be valued equally. This shift promotes psychological well-being, job satisfaction, and a sense of purpose.

Encouraging Work-Life Balance

By recognizing all forms of labor and compensating them equally, Kalkiism encourages a healthier work-life balance. With financial security no longer tied to overwork or high-income professions, individuals can allocate time to personal growth, leisure, and community engagement.

Hypothetical Scenarios: Fairness and Productivity in Action

To illustrate the principles of Kalkiism, let us explore hypothetical scenarios that demonstrate its impact on fairness and productivity.

Scenario 1: The Farmer and the Artist

In a small Kalkiist community, a farmer and an artist both contribute eight hours of labor each day. The farmer grows crops that feed the community, while the artist creates murals that beautify public spaces and uplift morale.

Under a traditional economy, the farmer's work might be undervalued due to fluctuating crop prices, while the artist might struggle to find buyers for their work. In a Kalkiist economy, both individuals earn eight hours of time credits, reflecting the equal value of their contributions. This ensures that both the farmer and the artist can meet their needs and continue to enrich the community.

Scenario 2: The Surgeon and the Caregiver

A surgeon performs life-saving operations, while a caregiver spends their days tending to elderly patients in a residential home. Both roles are essential to the health and well-being of society, yet in traditional systems, their compensation is vastly different.

In a Kalkiist economy, the surgeon and the caregiver earn the same hourly wage. This does not diminish the importance of the surgeon's specialized skills but rather acknowledges the equal importance of compassionate care. As a result, both individuals are valued and supported, creating a more inclusive and equitable society.

Scenario 3: The Young Innovator

A young entrepreneur in a Kalkiist society develops an innovative solution for renewable energy. In a traditional economy, their success might depend on securing funding or navigating competitive markets. In a Kalkiist economy, the innovator is supported through collaboration and community resources, earning time credits for their work regardless of immediate profitability. This system fosters innovation by removing financial barriers and emphasizing collective progress.

Fairness and Productivity: A Synergistic Relationship

One of the most compelling aspects of Kalkiism is its ability to balance fairness with productivity. Critics of equal hourly wages often argue that such systems discourage ambition or fail to reward exceptional contributions. However, Kalkiism demonstrates that fairness and productivity are not mutually exclusive; in fact, they reinforce each other.

By ensuring that all workers are valued equally, Kalkiism motivates individuals to contribute their best efforts without fear of exploitation. Productivity flourishes in an environment where collaboration is prioritized over competition and where individuals are free to pursue meaningful work.

Moreover, Kalkiism's inclusive approach to labor ensures that all resources—human and otherwise—are utilized efficiently. By compensating caregiving, household management, and other undervalued roles, Kalkiism maximizes societal contributions and eliminates the inefficiencies of unpaid labor.

Conclusion

Kalkiism redefines work and value by embracing inclusivity, promoting equality, and fostering dignity. Through its recognition of all forms of labor and its revolutionary approach to wages, Kalkiism challenges the inequities of traditional systems and offers a vision of fairness and productivity.

By valuing household management and caregiving, Kalkiism acknowledges the vital contributions that sustain society. By standardizing wages across professions, it dismantles hierarchies and promotes social cohesion. Through hypothetical scenarios, it demonstrates the practicality and impact of its principles.

Ultimately, Kalkiism's redefinition of work and value represents a profound shift in societal priorities. It offers not only a new economic framework but also a new way of understanding and appreciating the contributions of every individual. In doing so, Kalkiism lays the foundation for a more equitable, inclusive, and harmonious world.

Chapter 4: Building the Kalkiist Market

A market is the heartbeat of any economic system, a dynamic arena where goods, services, and ideas flow. In traditional economies, markets are defined by the movement of money, serving as both a medium of exchange and a measure of value. However, these monetary systems often perpetuate inequality, limit access to basic necessities, and incentivize exploitation. Kalkiism presents a bold alternative: a time-based economy where time is the sole currency. This chapter explores how vibrant markets function within this framework, how supply and demand operate without traditional money, and the mechanisms Kalkiism employs to ensure abundance and prevent scarcity.

The Role of Vibrant Markets in a Time-Based Economy

Markets in a Kalkiist economy are as vibrant and dynamic as those in traditional economies but are fundamentally more equitable. By replacing monetary currency with time units, Kalkiism democratizes markets, granting every individual equal purchasing power and ensuring fair access to goods and services.

Equality in Participation

Traditional markets often exclude those without sufficient financial resources, creating disparities in access to essentials such as food, healthcare, and education. In a Kalkiist market, every individual's time is valued equally, enabling universal participation. Whether one is a farmer, artist, teacher, or caregiver, their time credits hold the same purchasing power, fostering inclusivity and reducing social hierarchies.

Encouraging Collaboration and Innovation

Kalkiist markets encourage collaboration over competition. Since profit maximization is no longer the primary goal, individuals and enterprises focus on optimizing processes and improving the quality of goods and services. The emphasis on cooperation leads to a more innovative and sustainable economy, where creativity thrives without the constraints of financial barriers.

Fostering Local and Global Connections

While rooted in local communities, Kalkiist markets are inherently adaptable to global networks. Digital platforms facilitate the exchange of goods and services across regions, ensuring that surplus resources in one area can address shortages in another. This interconnectedness enhances efficiency and strengthens global solidarity.

Supply and Demand Without Traditional Currency

One of the key challenges of a time-based economy is ensuring that supply and demand function effectively without the use of money. Kalkiism addresses this by redefining how value is assigned and how market dynamics operate.

Time-Based Pricing

In Kalkiist markets, the price of goods and services is determined by the time required to produce or deliver them. For example, a loaf of bread might cost two hours, reflecting the cumulative time spent growing wheat, milling flour, and baking. This straightforward pricing model ensures transparency and fairness, aligning the cost of items with the labor involved.

Balancing Supply and Demand

Supply and demand in a time-based economy are regulated through collective planning and decentralized decision-making. Communities assess their needs and allocate resources accordingly, minimizing waste and ensuring that production aligns with actual demand.

For instance, if a community requires a certain quantity of rice, farmers collectively determine how much to cultivate, taking into account factors such as labor availability, environmental conditions, and storage capacity. Digital tools and algorithms assist in tracking consumption patterns and forecasting future needs, enabling precise adjustments to supply.

Eliminating Speculation and Hoarding

Traditional markets are often distorted by speculation and hoarding, where individuals or corporations manipulate supply to drive up prices. In a Kalkiist economy, such practices are rendered obsolete. Since time credits cannot be accumulated as wealth or used for exploitation, there is no incentive to hoard resources. This ensures a steady flow of goods and services, maintaining stability in the market.

Mechanisms for Ensuring Abundance and Avoiding Scarcity

The success of any economic system depends on its ability to provide for the needs of its population. Kalkiism incorporates several mechanisms to ensure abundance while preventing scarcity, promoting a resilient and sustainable economy.

1. Prioritizing Basic Needs

The cornerstone of Kalkiism is the Gross Domestic Requirement (GDR), which identifies the resources and services necessary to meet the population's basic needs. These include food, shelter, healthcare, education, and energy. By focusing on sufficiency rather than excess, Kalkiist markets allocate resources efficiently and equitably, ensuring that everyone has access to essentials.

For example, agricultural production is prioritized to ensure food security. Farmers earn time credits for their labor, and the resulting produce is distributed through local markets at time-based prices. This system guarantees that no one goes hungry, while excess production is stored or shared with neighboring communities.

2. Community-Centered Planning

While Kalkiist markets are decentralized, they rely on community input to guide production and distribution. Local councils or cooperatives assess the needs of their populations and coordinate with producers to meet these demands. This participatory approach empowers communities, fosters accountability, and prevents overproduction or underutilization of resources.

3. Leveraging Technology for Resource Management

Advances in technology play a critical role in ensuring abundance in a Kalkiist economy. Digital platforms track the availability and consumption of goods and services in real time, enabling precise adjustments to supply. For instance, sensors and data analytics in agriculture can monitor crop yields and predict shortages, allowing for timely interventions.

Blockchain technology, with its secure and transparent ledger system, facilitates the exchange of time credits and ensures accountability in transactions. Artificial intelligence and machine learning further optimize resource allocation, identifying inefficiencies and suggesting improvements.

4. Encouraging Diverse Production

Kalkiist markets promote diverse production to enhance resilience and prevent dependency on a single source or product. By encouraging local industries and small-scale enterprises, Kalkiism reduces the risk of supply chain disruptions and creates a more self-sufficient economy.

For example, a community might support multiple farmers growing different crops, ensuring a varied diet and reducing the risk of food shortages caused by crop failure. Similarly, local artisans and manufacturers contribute to a balanced market, offering goods and services tailored to community needs.

5. Addressing Environmental Sustainability

Kalkiist markets prioritize sustainability, recognizing that abundance must not come at the expense of the environment. Production methods are designed to minimize waste, conserve resources, and reduce carbon footprints. Renewable energy sources power industries, and circular economy principles ensure that materials are reused and recycled.

For example, a Kalkiist textile industry might focus on producing durable clothing using eco-friendly materials. Garments are repaired and repurposed when possible, reducing the need for excessive production and minimizing environmental impact.

6. Redistribution of Surpluses

In cases of surplus, Kalkiist markets emphasize redistribution to prevent waste and address shortages elsewhere. Time credits facilitate these exchanges, enabling communities with excess resources to share them with those in need. For instance, a region experiencing a bumper harvest of fruits might distribute the surplus to neighboring areas, ensuring that no food goes to waste.

Hypothetical Scenarios: The Kalkiist Market in Action

Scenario 1: A Local Market in a Rural Community

In a rural Kalkiist community, farmers, artisans, and service providers gather at a local market. A farmer sells vegetables, earning time credits that they use to purchase handmade furniture from a carpenter. The carpenter, in turn, uses those credits to access healthcare services. This seamless exchange highlights the vibrancy and fairness of a Kalkiist market, where everyone's contributions are valued equally.

Scenario 2: Addressing a Shortage

A coastal community faces a temporary shortage of fish due to environmental factors. Using digital platforms, the community requests assistance from neighboring regions with surplus fish. The exchange is facilitated through time credits, ensuring a smooth transfer of resources. This collaborative approach prevents scarcity and strengthens inter-community ties.

Scenario 3: Encouraging Innovation

An inventor in a Kalkiist society develops a new water filtration system. They earn time credits for their work, which is funded collectively by the community. The system is then manufactured locally, providing clean water at an affordable cost (measured in time) to all residents. This scenario illustrates how Kalkiist markets incentivize innovation while ensuring accessibility and affordability.

Transforming Markets for a Just Society

The Kalkiist market represents a radical departure from traditional economic systems, offering a framework that prioritizes equality, sustainability, and abundance. By replacing money with time, Kalkiism eliminates the disparities and inefficiencies of monetary markets, creating a system where everyone's contributions are valued and rewarded.

Through time-based pricing, community-centered planning, and advanced technology, Kalkiist markets balance supply and demand with precision and fairness. Mechanisms such as surplus redistribution, diverse production, and environmental sustainability ensure resilience and abundance, preventing scarcity and fostering harmony.

Ultimately, the Kalkiist market is more than an economic model; it is a vision of a society where cooperation and inclusivity replace competition and inequality. It offers a blueprint for a future where prosperity is shared, and every individual's time and effort are valued equally.

Chapter 5: Democracy Redefined

Democracy, at its core, promises equality, freedom, and representation. Yet, in practice, traditional democracies are often undermined by economic hierarchies that concentrate power in the hands of the wealthy. The influence of money on politics skews decision-making, perpetuates inequality, and disenfranchises marginalized communities. Kalkiism reimagines democracy by addressing these flaws at their root. By eliminating economic hierarchies and fostering true equality, Kalkiism creates a system where political power is distributed equitably, decision-making is transparent, and corruption is effectively neutralized. In doing so, Kalkiism redefines democracy, aligning it with its original ideals and paving the way for a more inclusive and just society.

Kalkiism as a Driver of True Democracy

The central premise of Kalkiism is the replacement of traditional currency with time as the universal measure of value. This shift eliminates the disparities created by wealth accumulation and establishes a foundation of economic equality. In a Kalkiist society, every individual earns the same hourly wage for their labor, regardless of their profession, and uses time credits to access goods and services. This economic structure directly translates into a more equitable political system.

Eliminating Economic Hierarchies

In capitalist democracies, wealth often dictates political influence. Campaign financing, lobbying, and media ownership enable the wealthy to shape policies and agendas to serve their interests, sidelining the voices of ordinary citizens. Kalkiism removes this imbalance by standardizing income and eradicating financial wealth as a source of power.

With economic hierarchies dismantled, every individual has equal standing in the political arena. Elections are no longer swayed by massive campaign donations, and policies are shaped by the collective needs of the population rather than the priorities of the elite. This democratization of economic power ensures that political representation is truly reflective of the people.

Fostering Participatory Governance

Kalkiism also emphasizes participatory governance, where citizens actively contribute to decision-making processes. Local councils, comprised of representatives chosen by their communities, collaborate to address collective needs and allocate resources. This grassroots approach ensures that governance is inclusive and responsive, empowering individuals to have a direct say in the policies that affect their lives.

Economic Equality as the Foundation for Political and Social Equity

Economic inequality is a primary driver of political and social disparities. When wealth is concentrated in the hands of a few, access to education, healthcare, and opportunities becomes uneven, perpetuating cycles of poverty and exclusion. Kalkiism's commitment to economic equality disrupts these cycles, fostering a society where everyone has an equal chance to thrive.

Enhancing Political Equity

Economic equality under Kalkiism ensures that no individual or group wields disproportionate influence over political processes. Equal wages and time-based currency create a level playing field, where every citizen's voice carries the same weight. Political campaigns are publicly funded using time credits, removing the need for private donations and eliminating the corrupting influence of money in politics.

Promoting Social Equity

Kalkiism recognizes that social equity is intrinsically tied to economic fairness. By compensating all forms of labor equally, Kalkiism values contributions such as caregiving, household management, and community service, which are often marginalized in traditional economies. This inclusive approach reduces gender disparities, uplifts marginalized communities, and fosters a culture of mutual respect.

For example, a Kalkiist society ensures that a single mother caring for her children has the same access to education and healthcare as a corporate executive. This universal access to resources breaks down social hierarchies and strengthens the social fabric.

Building Trust and Solidarity

Economic equality also nurtures trust and solidarity among citizens. When everyone is assured of their basic needs and recognized for their contributions, divisions based on class, race, or gender are diminished. This shared sense of purpose and belonging reinforces the democratic values of unity and cooperation.

Mechanisms to Prevent Corruption and Ensure Transparency

Corruption is one of the greatest threats to democracy, eroding trust in institutions and undermining public confidence. In traditional systems, corruption often arises from the intersection of wealth and power, with individuals using financial resources to manipulate outcomes for personal gain. Kalkiism addresses this issue through structural reforms and technological innovations that prioritize transparency, accountability, and fairness.

1. Decentralized Decision-Making

Kalkiism decentralizes governance, empowering local councils and community assemblies to make decisions collaboratively. This participatory approach minimizes the concentration of power and reduces the likelihood of corruption. By involving citizens directly in decision-making, Kalkiism fosters accountability and ensures that policies reflect the collective will.

2. Transparent Resource Allocation

In a Kalkiist economy, resources are allocated based on Gross Domestic Requirement (GDR), a metric that identifies the needs of the population. This transparent and data-driven approach eliminates opportunities for favoritism or mismanagement. For example, healthcare resources are distributed according to community needs rather than the ability to pay, ensuring equitable access for all.

3. Technology for Accountability

Advanced technology plays a critical role in preventing corruption and enhancing transparency in a Kalkiist society. Blockchain, with its secure and tamper-proof ledger system, records all transactions and decisions, providing a transparent record accessible to all citizens. This system ensures that time credits, resource allocations, and governance decisions are tracked and verifiable.

For instance, if a local council allocates resources for infrastructure development, the blockchain record details how time credits are spent, who is involved, and the outcomes achieved. This transparency discourages misuse of resources and builds public trust.

4. Public Campaign Financing

Political campaigns in a Kalkiist democracy are publicly funded using time credits, removing the influence of private donations. Candidates receive equal time credits to communicate their platforms, ensuring a fair and level playing field. This system prioritizes the quality of ideas over the quantity of resources, enabling citizens to make informed choices based on merit.

5. Whistleblower Protections and Oversight

Kalkiism establishes robust mechanisms for oversight and accountability, including independent auditing bodies and whistleblower protections. Citizens are encouraged to report unethical behavior without fear of retaliation, fostering a culture of integrity and transparency.

Hypothetical Scenarios: Democracy in a Kalkiist Society

Scenario 1: Participatory Budgeting

In a Kalkiist city, residents gather for a community assembly to decide how time credits should be allocated for public projects. Using digital tools, citizens vote on proposals, such as building a new school or expanding renewable energy infrastructure. The transparent process ensures that resources are directed toward the community's priorities, reflecting the democratic will.

Scenario 2: Transparent Governance

A local council in a rural area oversees the distribution of agricultural resources. Blockchain technology records every decision, from the allocation of seeds to the distribution of harvested crops. Citizens can access these records, ensuring that resources are used efficiently and fairly.

Scenario 3: Equal Political Representation

In a national election, candidates receive equal time credits to run their campaigns. Debates are broadcast on public platforms, and citizens evaluate candidates based on their policies and vision rather than their financial backing. This system ensures that elections are decided by ideas, not wealth.

Democracy Aligned with Its True Ideals

Kalkiism redefines democracy by eliminating the distortions caused by economic inequality and wealth-driven politics. Its time-based economy, equal wages, and transparent governance create a system where political power is genuinely distributed among the people.

By addressing the root causes of corruption, empowering citizens through participatory governance, and fostering social and economic equity, Kalkiism aligns democracy with its original ideals of equality, freedom, and representation. It offers a vision of a society where every individual has an equal voice and every contribution is valued.

As humanity confronts the challenges of inequality, polarization, and environmental crises, Kalkiism provides a blueprint for a more inclusive, transparent, and just democracy. It is not merely a redefinition of governance but a reimagining of society itself—one that prioritizes fairness, unity, and the shared pursuit of progress.

Chapter 6: Innovation and the Cambrian Explosion of Productivity

Human innovation is the driving force behind progress, shaping civilizations and addressing global challenges. Yet, traditional economic systems often stifle innovation, either by concentrating resources in the hands of a few or by discouraging risk-taking in favor of immediate profits. Kalkiism offers an alternative framework that fosters creativity and productivity by emphasizing cooperation, equality, and shared purpose. By replacing monetary systems with time as the universal currency and ensuring economic equity, Kalkiism lays the foundation for a Cambrian explosion of innovation—an unprecedented era of breakthroughs in technology, art, and science.

Unprecedented Human Cooperation

The cornerstone of Kalkiism's approach to fostering innovation is its emphasis on human cooperation. In capitalist systems, competition often pits individuals and organizations against one another, prioritizing short-term gains over long-term solutions. This adversarial model can create inefficiencies, duplicate efforts, and exclude talented individuals who lack financial resources or access to networks.

Kalkiism, on the other hand, transforms the economic landscape by removing barriers to collaboration. In a time-based economy, where all labor is equally valued, individuals and organizations are incentivized to work together rather than compete. Cooperation becomes the driving force behind progress, as shared goals and mutual respect replace the profit motive.

Shared Purpose and Collective Goals

Kalkiism encourages societies to focus on collective well-being rather than individual accumulation of wealth. Communities work together to identify and address pressing challenges, from climate change to public health. This collective approach pools resources, talent, and expertise, creating an environment where innovative solutions can thrive.

For example, a community might collaboratively develop renewable energy technologies, with scientists, engineers, and local workers contributing their skills. Each participant earns time credits for their efforts, ensuring that everyone's contributions are valued equally.

Removing Barriers to Entry

In a Kalkiist society, access to education, training, and resources is universal, ensuring that talent and creativity are not constrained by socioeconomic status. A young inventor in a rural area has the same opportunities to develop their ideas as a seasoned researcher in an urban center. This inclusivity unleashes the full potential of human ingenuity, bringing diverse perspectives and ideas into the innovation process.

Breakthroughs in Technology, Art, and Science

The collaborative and egalitarian nature of Kalkiism creates fertile ground for transformative breakthroughs across disciplines. By aligning resources with societal needs and valuing all contributions equally, Kalkiism accelerates progress in technology, art, and science.

Technological Advancements

Kalkiism's emphasis on cooperation and shared resources paves the way for groundbreaking technological innovations. In a time-based economy, projects are driven by collective benefit rather than profit, enabling bold and ambitious endeavors.

1. **Renewable Energy**: Communities in a Kalkiist society invest in renewable energy technologies, such as solar panels, wind turbines, and advanced energy storage systems. By pooling expertise and resources, they create sustainable energy solutions that benefit everyone.

2. **Space Exploration**: Freed from financial constraints, collaborative teams of scientists and engineers work on interplanetary exploration and colonization. Time credits reward their efforts, ensuring equitable recognition for all contributors.

3. **Medical Technology**: In a Kalkiist healthcare system, researchers prioritize breakthroughs in diagnostics, treatments, and preventative care. From curing diseases to developing affordable medical devices, innovation focuses on improving quality of life rather than generating profits.

Artistic Flourishes

In a Kalkiist society, art is celebrated as an essential expression of human creativity. The equal valuation of all labor enables artists to pursue their passions without financial pressure, fostering a cultural renaissance.

1. **Public Art and Architecture**: Communities commission artists and architects to create spaces that inspire and uplift. Murals, sculptures, and eco-friendly buildings become integral to public life, reflecting shared values and aspirations.

2. **Cultural Diversity**: By removing financial barriers, Kalkiism enables artists from diverse backgrounds to share their perspectives. This inclusivity enriches cultural landscapes, promoting mutual understanding and appreciation.

3. **New Media and Digital Art**: With access to technology and resources, creators experiment with virtual reality, artificial intelligence, and other emerging media. These innovations push the boundaries of artistic expression, engaging audiences in novel ways.

Scientific Discoveries

Kalkiism prioritizes scientific research as a cornerstone of progress. By ensuring equitable access to resources and recognizing the value of all contributions, Kalkiist societies cultivate environments where scientific breakthroughs flourish.

1. **Climate Solutions**: Researchers collaborate to develop technologies that mitigate climate change, from carbon capture systems to sustainable agriculture practices. These efforts are driven by collective responsibility and shared goals.

2. **Healthcare Innovations**: Kalkiism's emphasis on equality ensures that medical research addresses global health challenges rather than focusing on profit-driven areas. Vaccines, treatments, and public health strategies benefit populations worldwide.

3. **Fundamental Research**: Freed from the need to justify immediate financial returns, scientists pursue fundamental questions about the universe, laying the groundwork for future applications. Discoveries in physics, biology, and

other fields expand humanity's understanding of the world.

The Interplay of Freedom and Equality in Fostering Innovation

Kalkiism's unique balance of freedom and equality creates an ideal environment for innovation. While individuals are free to pursue their passions and explore creative ideas, the system's emphasis on equity ensures that everyone has the tools and support they need to succeed.

Freedom to Experiment

In a Kalkiist economy, failure is not penalized as it often is in traditional systems. Innovators are free to take risks and experiment with new ideas without fear of financial ruin. This freedom encourages bold thinking and accelerates the development of groundbreaking solutions.

For instance, an inventor working on an ambitious renewable energy project receives time credits for their efforts, regardless of the project's immediate success. This support allows them to refine their ideas and contribute to long-term progress.

Equality of Opportunity

Kalkiism's commitment to economic equality ensures that everyone, regardless of background, has access to education, training, and resources. This inclusivity brings diverse perspectives to the innovation process, fostering creativity and resilience.

Consider a young artist in a Kalkiist society who dreams of creating large-scale installations. With access to materials, mentorship, and collaborative networks, they can bring their vision to life, enriching their community and inspiring others.

Collaboration Over Competition

The cooperative ethos of Kalkiism replaces cutthroat competition with collaboration. Innovators work together to address shared challenges, pooling knowledge and resources to achieve collective goals.

For example, a team of researchers from different disciplines might collaborate on a project to develop biodegradable packaging. By combining expertise in materials science, design, and sustainability, they create a product that benefits society and the environment.

Hypothetical Scenarios: A Glimpse into Kalkiist Innovation

Scenario 1: A Renewable Energy Revolution

In a Kalkiist society, communities across the globe collaborate on renewable energy projects. Engineers, scientists, and local workers develop solar farms, wind turbines, and hydropower systems tailored to regional needs. The resulting energy infrastructure provides clean, affordable power to all, reducing reliance on fossil fuels and mitigating climate change.

Scenario 2: An Artistic Renaissance

Freed from financial constraints, artists in a Kalkiist city transform public spaces into vibrant hubs of creativity. Sculptures, murals, and interactive installations reflect the community's history and aspirations. These projects foster civic pride and attract visitors, enriching the cultural fabric of the city.

Scenario 3: Breakthroughs in Healthcare

A Kalkiist healthcare system prioritizes research into rare diseases, neglected conditions, and preventative care. Collaborative teams of scientists and physicians develop affordable treatments and vaccines, ensuring equitable access to lifesaving innovations.

A New Era of Human Potential

Kalkiism's emphasis on cooperation, equality, and shared purpose creates an economic environment where innovation flourishes. By removing barriers to collaboration, valuing all contributions equally, and ensuring universal access to resources, Kalkiism unleashes the full potential of human creativity and ingenuity.

This Cambrian explosion of productivity has far-reaching implications, driving breakthroughs in technology, art, and science that benefit humanity as a whole. The interplay of freedom and equality fosters a culture of bold thinking and collaboration, laying the foundation for a future defined by progress and shared prosperity.

Kalkiism is not just an economic system—it is a framework for realizing humanity's highest aspirations. By aligning innovation with the principles of fairness and cooperation, it offers a vision of a world where creativity knows no bounds and every individual has the opportunity to contribute to a brighter future.

Chapter 7: Eliminating Poverty and Scarcity

Poverty and scarcity have plagued humanity for centuries, with billions lacking access to basic needs such as food, shelter, and healthcare. Traditional economic systems—whether capitalist or communist—have failed to provide universal prosperity. While capitalism fosters wealth accumulation for a few, it leaves many in poverty. Communism, despite its promises of equality, often results in inefficiency, scarcity, and authoritarian control. Kalkiism offers a fundamentally different approach, eradicating poverty and scarcity through its innovative Gross Domestic Requirement (GDR) framework, time-based currency, and egalitarian principles. This chapter explores how Kalkiism raises living standards universally, addresses the challenges of global implementation, and compares its effectiveness with that of capitalism and communism.

Kalkiism's Framework for Eradicating Poverty

At the core of Kalkiism's solution to poverty and scarcity is its emphasis on meeting the Gross Domestic Requirement (GDR) of every individual and community. Unlike Gross Domestic Product (GDP), which measures economic output without considering distribution, GDR focuses on ensuring that everyone has access to essential resources and services. This paradigm shift prioritizes sufficiency over profit, aligning economic activity with human needs.

Basic Needs as a Right

Kalkiism guarantees universal access to basic necessities, including food, housing, healthcare, education, and energy. These essentials are no longer treated as commodities subject to market fluctuations but as rights guaranteed to all individuals. By replacing monetary wealth with time as the universal currency, Kalkiism eliminates financial barriers to these necessities, ensuring equitable access for everyone.

For instance, a single mother in a Kalkiist society earns time credits for her caregiving work. She uses these credits to secure housing, access nutritious food, and provide education for her children. Her contributions are recognized and valued equally to those of a surgeon or engineer, affirming her dignity and ensuring her family's well-being.

Efficient Resource Allocation

The GDR framework ensures that resources are distributed according to need, minimizing waste and preventing shortages. Communities assess their requirements collaboratively, using data-driven tools to allocate resources effectively. This collective planning approach prevents overproduction, hoarding, and exploitation, which are common in traditional economic systems.

For example, if a region experiences a surplus of agricultural produce, the excess is redistributed to areas facing shortages. This system eliminates food waste and ensures that no one goes hungry, demonstrating Kalkiism's commitment to abundance and fairness.

Raising Living Standards Universally

Kalkiism's time-based economy and emphasis on equality create a foundation for universally improved living standards. By valuing all labor equally and prioritizing collective well-being, Kalkiism ensures that everyone benefits from economic progress.

Universal Healthcare and Education

In a Kalkiist society, healthcare and education are universally accessible. Doctors, teachers, and other professionals earn time credits for their work, and their services are available to all without financial barriers. This model ensures high-quality care and education for everyone, regardless of their social or economic status.

For example, a child born in a remote village has the same opportunities for education as one in an urban center. Access to technology, skilled teachers, and resources enables them to achieve their potential, contributing to societal progress.

Housing and Infrastructure

Kalkiism prioritizes the construction of affordable, sustainable housing and infrastructure. Architects, engineers, and construction workers are compensated in time credits, and housing is allocated based on need rather than market prices. This system eliminates homelessness and ensures that everyone lives in safe, comfortable conditions.

Environmental Sustainability

By integrating sustainable practices into its economic framework, Kalkiism ensures that improved living standards do not come at the expense of the environment. Renewable energy, waste reduction, and conservation efforts are prioritized, creating a harmonious balance between human development and ecological health.

Challenges and Solutions in Implementing GDR Globally

The transition to Kalkiism and the implementation of GDR at a global scale present significant challenges. However, these obstacles can be addressed through careful planning, international cooperation, and technological innovation.

1. Resistance to Change

Many individuals and institutions may resist Kalkiism due to vested interests in the existing economic systems. Wealthy elites, corporations, and political leaders who benefit from capitalism may oppose the redistribution of resources and the abolition of monetary wealth.

Solution: Education and awareness campaigns can help build public support for Kalkiism by highlighting its benefits and addressing misconceptions. Pilot programs in communities and regions can demonstrate the system's effectiveness, creating momentum for broader adoption.

2. Global Coordination

Implementing GDR requires international cooperation to address disparities between countries and ensure equitable resource distribution. Developing nations may face challenges in adopting the system due to existing infrastructure and resource constraints.

Solution: Wealthier nations can support the transition by sharing technology, expertise, and resources. International organizations can facilitate coordination, ensuring that GDR implementation aligns with global goals for sustainability and equity.

3. Technological Integration

A Kalkiist economy relies on advanced technology for tracking time credits, resource allocation, and decision-making. Ensuring universal access to these technologies is critical.

Solution: Investments in digital infrastructure, open-source software, and training programs can ensure that all communities have access to the tools needed for a Kalkiist economy. Blockchain technology can provide secure, transparent systems for managing time credits and resource distribution.

4. Cultural Adaptation

Cultural differences and historical contexts may influence how Kalkiism is received in different regions. Some communities may be skeptical of its principles or find aspects of the system challenging to integrate with their traditions.

Solution: Kalkiism should be adapted to local contexts, respecting cultural values and traditions. Community involvement in the design and implementation process ensures that the system reflects the needs and priorities of diverse populations.

Comparing Kalkiism with Capitalism and Communism

Kalkiism represents a radical departure from both capitalism and communism, addressing the shortcomings of each while offering a new vision for eradicating poverty and scarcity.

Capitalism's Shortcomings

Capitalism has been effective in generating wealth and fostering innovation, but it fails to distribute resources equitably. Income inequality, exploitation, and environmental degradation are persistent issues. Under capitalism, essential services such as healthcare and education are often inaccessible to the poor, perpetuating cycles of poverty.

Kalkiism counters these flaws by prioritizing equality and universal access. By replacing profit-driven motives with time-based incentives, Kalkiism eliminates exploitation and ensures that progress benefits everyone.

Communism's Limitations

Communism sought to address inequality by abolishing private property and centralizing economic control. However, this approach often resulted in inefficiency, scarcity, and authoritarian governance. The lack of incentives for productivity and innovation hindered progress, while centralized control stifled individual freedom.

Kalkiism avoids these pitfalls by combining equality with freedom. Its decentralized, community-driven approach empowers individuals while fostering collaboration. The time-based economy ensures fair compensation without sacrificing productivity or creativity.

A New Paradigm

Kalkiism transcends the binary opposition of capitalism and communism, offering a system that values both individual contributions and collective well-being. By aligning economic activity with human needs and environmental sustainability,

Kalkiism provides a holistic framework for eradicating poverty and scarcity.

Hypothetical Scenarios: Kalkiism in Action

Scenario 1: A Self-Sustaining Community

In a rural Kalkiist community, residents collaborate to produce food, build housing, and provide education. Farmers earn time credits for their labor, which they use to access healthcare and other services. The community's needs are met through collective planning, ensuring that everyone thrives.

Scenario 2: Global Resource Sharing

A drought in one region threatens food security, but neighboring areas with surplus crops share their resources. Blockchain technology facilitates the exchange of time credits, ensuring transparency and fairness. This cooperation prevents hunger and reinforces global solidarity.

Scenario 3: Universal Healthcare Access

In a Kalkiist city, a hospital provides free healthcare to all residents. Doctors, nurses, and support staff earn time credits for their work, which they use to access housing, education, and leisure activities. Patients receive high-quality care without financial barriers, demonstrating the system's commitment to equity.

A Future Without Poverty or Scarcity

Kalkiism offers a transformative vision of a world where poverty and scarcity are eradicated, and living standards are universally improved. Through its GDR framework, time-based economy, and commitment to equality, Kalkiism addresses the root causes of economic and social disparities.

By prioritizing basic needs, fostering cooperation, and leveraging technology, Kalkiism creates a system that benefits everyone, from individuals to entire communities. Its ability to adapt to diverse cultural contexts and address global challenges makes it a viable solution for the pressing issues of our time.

As humanity faces the interconnected crises of inequality, environmental degradation, and resource scarcity, Kalkiism provides a blueprint for a more equitable and sustainable future. It is not just an economic system but a paradigm shift that redefines progress, prosperity, and the human experience.

Chapter 8: A Day in the Life of a Kalkiist Society

Imagine a world where every individual's time is valued equally, where basic needs are universally guaranteed, and where cooperation replaces competition. This is the world of Kalkiism, a society driven by fairness, inclusivity, and sustainability. A day in a Kalkiist society showcases its transformative power, with vibrant markets, seamless transactions, and thriving communities. Through the personal stories of its citizens, we see how this system fosters harmony and empowers individuals to live fulfilling lives.

Morning: Community and Connection

The sun rises over the Kalkiist town of Harmony Valley, nestled between rolling hills and a river that powers the local hydroelectric plant. The air is filled with the hum of life, as residents prepare to start their day.

Amira, the Caregiver

Amira begins her day tending to elderly residents at the community care center. In a traditional economy, her work might be undervalued or unpaid, but in Harmony Valley, Amira earns time credits for every hour she spends assisting her neighbors. She helps one resident with their morning routine, shares stories with another, and organizes a group exercise session. Her work not only earns her time credits but also strengthens the bonds within the community.

By 9 a.m., Amira finishes her morning shift and heads to the market. Using her time credits, she purchases fresh vegetables, fruit, and bread, all priced transparently in minutes and hours. The simplicity of the transaction reflects the Kalkiist ethos: fairness and clarity in every exchange.

Midday: Vibrant Markets and Creativity

The town's market square is a bustling hub of activity, where farmers, artisans, and service providers gather to exchange goods and ideas.

Javier, the Farmer

Javier, a local farmer, sets up his stall at the market, displaying an array of produce: tomatoes, peppers, and sweet corn harvested that morning. His earnings in time credits reflect the labor he and his team invested in growing and harvesting the crops.

A nearby baker purchases Javier's corn to make cornbread, paying him with time credits. In turn, Javier uses his earnings to buy handcrafted pottery from a local artisan. The exchange is seamless, and every participant feels valued and connected.

Leila, the Artist

Leila, a painter and muralist, spends her morning sketching designs for a new public art installation. In a Kalkiist society, her work is recognized as vital to the community's cultural and aesthetic well-being. Later, she heads to the market to display her latest paintings, priced in hours based on the time she spent creating them.

A teacher purchases one of Leila's pieces for her classroom, using her time credits earned from teaching children. The transaction highlights the inclusive nature of the Kalkiist economy, where creativity and education are equally valued.

Afternoon: Collaboration and Innovation

Collaboration is at the heart of Kalkiism, driving innovation and progress across fields.

Dr. Noor, the Scientist

In the nearby research facility, Dr. Noor collaborates with a diverse team of scientists and engineers on a project to improve water purification technology. The team includes chemists, biologists, and local students, all earning time credits for their contributions.

Freed from the constraints of funding pressures and profit motives, the team focuses entirely on solving real-world problems. Their efforts are supported by the community, which recognizes the importance of clean water for health and sustainability.

The facility itself is powered by renewable energy, demonstrating the community's commitment to environmental stewardship. By evening, the team celebrates a breakthrough: a new filtration method that doubles the efficiency of existing systems.

Evening: Leisure and Learning

As the day winds down, residents gather to enjoy leisure activities and pursue personal growth.

Arjun, the Teacher

Arjun spends his evening leading a free workshop on sustainable gardening techniques. Residents earn time credits by participating, learning skills they can use to grow their own food. The workshop is held in the community center, a vibrant space that hosts classes, performances, and social events.

After the workshop, Arjun attends a poetry reading by Leila, who shares her latest work inspired by the town's natural beauty. The audience exchanges ideas and feedback, fostering a sense of connection and mutual respect.

Sofia, the Student

Sofia, a high school student, spends her evening volunteering at the local animal shelter. She earns time credits for her efforts, which she uses to access extracurricular activities like dance classes and music lessons. In a Kalkiist society, education and personal growth are prioritized, ensuring that every young person has the tools to succeed.

Harmony in Society

The day ends with a palpable sense of harmony and fulfillment. Kalkiism's principles are woven into every aspect of life in Harmony Valley, creating a society where cooperation, equity, and sustainability flourish.

Seamless Transactions

The simplicity of time-based transactions eliminates the stress and confusion often associated with traditional monetary systems. There are no hidden fees, interest rates, or financial hierarchies—just straightforward exchanges of time for goods and services.

Vibrant Markets

The market serves as more than a place for economic transactions; it is a hub of creativity and connection. Residents share stories, ideas, and innovations, strengthening the social fabric of the community.

Empowered Individuals

Every individual in Harmony Valley feels valued and empowered. Whether they are scientists, caregivers, artists, or farmers, their contributions are recognized and rewarded. This sense of equality fosters mutual respect and collaboration, driving progress in all areas of life.

Personal Stories: Thriving Under Kalkiism

Amira's Journey

Amira reflects on how her life has changed since the adoption of Kalkiism. In the old system, her caregiving work was unpaid, leaving her financially dependent and undervalued. Now, she earns time credits that provide for her family's needs while allowing her to pursue her passion for helping others.

Javier's Vision

Javier, the farmer, dreams of expanding his operations to include a community orchard. With the support of Kalkiist principles, he knows that his efforts will benefit not just his family but the entire town.

Leila's Legacy

Leila, the artist, takes pride in her work beautifying the town. Her murals inspire residents and attract visitors, enriching the community's cultural heritage.

Conclusion

A day in the life of a Kalkiist society reveals the transformative power of this economic and social framework. Through its emphasis on equality, cooperation, and sustainability, Kalkiism creates a world where everyone thrives. The simplicity of transactions, the vibrancy of markets, and the empowerment of individuals showcase the potential of Kalkiism to redefine how we live, work, and connect.

In this society, poverty and scarcity are relics of the past, replaced by abundance, fairness, and harmony. As humanity seeks solutions to the challenges of inequality and resource scarcity, Kalkiism offers a vision of a brighter, more inclusive future.

Chapter 9: Myths and Misconceptions

Every revolutionary idea faces skepticism and misunderstanding, and Kalkiism is no exception. As a fundamentally new economic and social framework, Kalkiism challenges entrenched notions of value, equity, and progress. Its innovative approach—replacing monetary systems with time as currency and prioritizing Gross Domestic Requirement (GDR) over Gross Domestic Product (GDP)—can be difficult for critics to grasp without resorting to comparisons with existing models. This chapter addresses common myths and misconceptions about Kalkiism, clarifies how it differs from capitalism and communism, and discusses the transition process, including potential challenges and solutions.

Myth 1: Kalkiism Is Just Another Form of Communism

A frequent critique of Kalkiism is that it resembles communism, with its focus on equality and the redistribution of resources. However, this comparison overlooks fundamental differences between the two systems.

Core Differences

Communism seeks to abolish private property and establish a classless society through centralized control of resources and production. Historically, this approach has often led to inefficiency, scarcity, and authoritarian governance, as state control concentrated power in the hands of a few.

Kalkiism, by contrast, maintains decentralization as a core principle. Rather than relying on centralized planning, it empowers communities to make decisions collaboratively. Resources are distributed based on GDR—a data-driven, transparent metric that ensures everyone's basic needs are met. Time-based currency replaces monetary wealth, ensuring that contributions to society are valued equally without sacrificing individual autonomy.

In a Kalkiist society, markets remain vibrant and dynamic, driven by cooperation rather than competition. Innovation and creativity are encouraged, as individuals are free to pursue their passions without the constraints of financial pressure or bureaucratic control.

Myth 2: Kalkiism Is a Reinvented Form of Capitalism

On the other end of the spectrum, some argue that Kalkiism retains elements of capitalism, such as markets and trade. However, this critique fails to recognize Kalkiism's fundamental break from capitalism's core tenets.

Core Differences

Capitalism is defined by private ownership, profit-driven motives, and competitive markets. While it has spurred significant technological advancements and economic growth, it has also perpetuated inequality, environmental degradation, and exploitation.

Kalkiism eliminates the profit motive, replacing it with time-based incentives that prioritize fairness and sustainability. Markets in a Kalkiist society operate without monetary currency, ensuring that goods and services are accessible to all. The emphasis shifts from maximizing wealth to fulfilling human needs and fostering collective well-being.

Where capitalism thrives on competition, Kalkiism thrives on cooperation. For example, instead of competing for resources, communities pool their skills and efforts to achieve shared goals. This collaborative ethos ensures that progress benefits everyone, not just the wealthy or powerful.

Myth 3: Kalkiism Will Lead to Laziness and Stagnation

Critics often claim that eliminating income disparities will remove the incentive to work, leading to laziness and stagnation. This misconception stems from traditional views that link productivity to financial rewards.

The Reality of Kalkiism

In a Kalkiist society, work is not merely a means of survival but a way to contribute meaningfully to the community. Time-based compensation ensures that all labor is valued equally, creating intrinsic motivation to participate in society.

Moreover, Kalkiism recognizes diverse forms of labor, including caregiving, community service, and creative pursuits, which are often undervalued in traditional systems. By valuing all contributions, Kalkiism fosters a culture of dignity and purpose, where individuals are motivated by respect, recognition, and the shared goal of improving collective well-being.

Innovation and Progress

Far from leading to stagnation, Kalkiism's cooperative framework encourages innovation. Freed from the constraints of financial pressures, individuals and teams can experiment, take risks, and pursue ambitious projects. The collaborative nature of Kalkiist markets ensures that breakthroughs in technology, art, and science benefit society as a whole.

Myth 4: Kalkiism Is Utopian and Unrealistic

Skeptics may view Kalkiism as an idealistic vision, detached from the complexities of real-world implementation. While it is ambitious, Kalkiism is grounded in practical principles and scalable mechanisms.

The Practical Foundation

Kalkiism's reliance on time as currency and GDR as an economic metric simplifies transactions and resource allocation. These concepts are supported by existing technologies, such as blockchain for tracking time credits and AI for optimizing resource distribution. Communities worldwide are already experimenting with similar ideas, from time-banking systems to local cooperative economies.

Incremental Implementation

Rather than proposing an overnight overhaul, Kalkiism advocates for gradual transition. Pilot programs in local communities can test its principles, refine its mechanisms, and build public support. Successful examples can then scale to regional and national levels, demonstrating its feasibility.

For example, a small town might adopt Kalkiist principles for specific sectors, such as healthcare or education. Over time, as the benefits become evident, the system expands to include broader aspects of the local economy.

Transition Challenges and Solutions

The journey toward a Kalkiist society is not without its challenges. Addressing these obstacles requires careful planning, global cooperation, and adaptability.

1. Resistance to Change

Many individuals and institutions benefit from the status quo and may resist the transition to Kalkiism.

Solution: Education and awareness campaigns can highlight Kalkiism's benefits and address concerns. Transparent communication and pilot programs can demonstrate the system's effectiveness and build trust.

2. Technological Infrastructure

Implementing a time-based economy and GDR framework requires advanced technological systems for tracking, allocation, and decision-making.

Solution: Investments in digital infrastructure, open-source tools, and training programs ensure accessibility. Collaborations between technologists and policymakers can design user-friendly systems that integrate seamlessly into daily life.

3. Cultural Differences

Kalkiism must adapt to diverse cultural contexts, respecting local traditions and values.

Solution: Community involvement in the design and implementation process ensures that Kalkiism aligns with cultural norms. Flexibility and inclusivity are key to addressing regional variations.

4. Global Cooperation

Coordinating the transition across nations with varying levels of development and resources poses a significant challenge.

Solution: International organizations and agreements can facilitate resource sharing, technological support, and knowledge exchange. Wealthier nations can assist developing countries in adopting Kalkiist principles, fostering global solidarity.

Why Kalkiism Works

Kalkiism's strength lies in its ability to address the flaws of both capitalism and communism while offering a practical and equitable alternative.

- **It Values Everyone Equally**: By replacing monetary wealth with time as currency, Kalkiism ensures that all contributions are recognized and rewarded.
- **It Prioritizes Needs Over Profits**: GDR aligns economic activity with human well-being, eliminating waste and inefficiency.
- **It Encourages Collaboration**: Kalkiism's cooperative ethos fosters innovation, progress, and social cohesion.
- **It Promotes Sustainability**: By integrating environmental stewardship into its framework, Kalkiism ensures that progress does not come at the expense of future generations.

Conclusion

Myths and misconceptions about Kalkiism often stem from comparisons to existing systems or misunderstandings of its principles. By addressing these critiques and clarifying its distinctions from capitalism and communism, Kalkiism emerges as a transformative framework with the potential to eradicate poverty, foster equality, and create a sustainable future.

The path to a Kalkiist society is not without challenges, but through education, collaboration, and incremental implementation, these obstacles can be overcome. Kalkiism is not utopian; it is a practical and scalable solution to the pressing issues of inequality, scarcity, and environmental degradation.

As humanity seeks new models for progress, Kalkiism offers a vision of a world where everyone thrives—where innovation flourishes, resources are shared equitably, and dignity is universal. It is a vision worth pursuing, and with commitment and cooperation, it is a vision that can become reality.

Chapter 10: A New World Order

The world as we know it is marked by profound inequality, environmental crises, and geopolitical tensions. Economic disparities between nations fuel conflict, limit progress, and perpetuate cycles of poverty. At the same time, the unchecked pursuit of profit has led to the exploitation of resources and people, endangering the planet's future. Kalkiism, as a revolutionary economic and social framework, offers a bold alternative—a global system based on equity, sustainability, and cooperation. This chapter explores the transformative potential of Kalkiism, its implications for international relations, and the pathway toward a new world order that transcends the divisions of the past.

Global Implications of Kalkiism

Adopting Kalkiism on a global scale would fundamentally reshape human society, addressing the root causes of inequality and fostering a culture of collaboration.

1. Eradicating Economic Disparities

Economic inequality between nations is one of the most significant challenges of our time. Wealthy countries dominate global trade and finance, while poorer nations struggle with debt, resource exploitation, and limited access to technology. Kalkiism, with its emphasis on Gross Domestic Requirement (GDR) and time-based currency, offers a framework for leveling the playing field.

Under Kalkiism, resources are distributed based on need rather than financial power. Developing nations gain access to the tools and expertise needed to meet their population's basic requirements, ensuring that no region is left behind. For example, surplus food from wealthier nations could be shared with regions experiencing scarcity, facilitated through transparent systems of time-based exchange.

2. Promoting Sustainability

Global challenges like climate change, deforestation, and water scarcity require collective action. Kalkiism's commitment to sustainability ensures that progress does not come at the expense of the planet. By prioritizing renewable energy, conservation, and resource efficiency, Kalkiist societies create a model for harmonious coexistence with nature.

For instance, international collaborations could focus on large-scale renewable energy projects, such as solar farms in sunny regions or wind turbines in coastal areas, benefiting multiple countries simultaneously. Time credits ensure that every contributor, regardless of nationality, is fairly compensated for their efforts.

3. Strengthening Peace and Stability

Economic disparities often drive conflict, as nations compete for resources and influence. Kalkiism addresses these tensions by promoting shared prosperity and interdependence. When every nation has the means to meet its needs, the incentive for war diminishes.

Furthermore, Kalkiism's emphasis on cooperation fosters mutual understanding and trust between nations. Cultural exchange, collaborative problem-solving, and equitable resource sharing lay the groundwork for a more peaceful world.

International Cooperation Under Kalkiism

The transition to Kalkiism requires unprecedented levels of international cooperation, as nations work together to implement its principles and overcome challenges.

1. Establishing Global Frameworks

A global Kalkiist order would necessitate the creation of international institutions to oversee the implementation of GDR, facilitate resource sharing, and monitor sustainability efforts. These institutions would operate transparently, ensuring that all nations have an equal voice in decision-making.

For example, a Global Resource Council could coordinate the distribution of surplus goods, while a Kalkiist Environmental Agency ensures that development aligns with ecological priorities.

2. Technology as a Unifying Tool

Advances in technology provide the infrastructure needed to implement Kalkiism on a global scale. Blockchain technology ensures transparent and secure time-credit transactions, while artificial intelligence optimizes resource allocation and consumption. Digital platforms enable real-time communication and collaboration between nations, fostering a sense of global community.

Imagine a scenario where scientists from multiple countries collaborate on a climate change solution, exchanging ideas and expertise through digital networks. Each participant earns time credits for their contributions, ensuring fair recognition and encouraging further cooperation.

3. Addressing Cultural Diversity

While Kalkiism offers universal principles, its implementation must respect cultural differences and local contexts. By involving communities in decision-making and tailoring solutions to regional needs, Kalkiism ensures that its benefits are inclusive and adaptable.

For instance, a rural community in Africa might prioritize agricultural development, while an urban center in Asia focuses on renewable energy infrastructure. Both approaches align with Kalkiism's goals, demonstrating its flexibility and inclusivity.

The Dissolution of Economic Disparities

Kalkiism not only addresses inequality within nations but also dismantles the economic hierarchies that divide the world.

1. Empowering Developing Nations

Developing nations often face systemic disadvantages, from debt burdens to exploitative trade practices. Kalkiism provides these nations with the resources and autonomy needed to thrive. By eliminating financial dependencies and focusing on mutual support, Kalkiism creates a global economy where every nation can flourish.

For example, instead of relying on foreign loans, a developing nation could implement a Kalkiist system that prioritizes local needs and resources. International partnerships provide technology and expertise, ensuring sustainable growth without exploitation.

2. Redefining Global Trade

Under Kalkiism, global trade is driven by cooperation rather than competition. Time-based exchange ensures that all participants are treated fairly, while GDR aligns trade priorities with human needs. This system eliminates exploitative practices, such as sweatshops or resource hoarding, fostering a more ethical and equitable global economy.

Imagine a scenario where farmers in Latin America exchange coffee with engineers in Europe, using time credits to facilitate the trade. Both parties benefit, and the transaction strengthens international ties.

Transitioning to a Kalkiist World Order

While the vision of a Kalkiist world is compelling, the path to its realization is complex. Transitioning from entrenched systems to a Kalkiist framework requires careful planning, global collaboration, and a commitment to shared values.

1. Pilot Programs and Regional Adoption

The transition begins with local and regional pilot programs that demonstrate Kalkiism's viability. Communities implement time-based economies and GDR frameworks, refining the model through practical experience. Successful programs serve as blueprints for larger-scale adoption.

For example, a city might adopt Kalkiist principles for its healthcare and education systems, ensuring universal access and equitable compensation. As residents experience the benefits, the system expands to include other sectors.

2. Building Public Support

Public understanding and acceptance are critical to Kalkiism's success. Education campaigns, community discussions, and transparent communication help build trust and address misconceptions. By involving citizens in the transition process, Kalkiism fosters a sense of ownership and engagement.

3. Overcoming Resistance

Entrenched interests, from corporations to political elites, may resist the shift to Kalkiism. Addressing this resistance requires strategic advocacy, legal frameworks, and grassroots mobilization. Demonstrating Kalkiism's benefits through tangible outcomes helps counter opposition.

A Vision for the Future

The global adoption of Kalkiism represents more than an economic shift; it is a transformation of human society. By prioritizing equity, sustainability, and cooperation, Kalkiism creates a world where everyone can thrive, regardless of their nationality or background.

Imagine a planet where no one goes hungry, where innovation benefits all, and where the environment is cherished rather than exploited. A world where nations collaborate rather than compete, and where the dignity of every individual is recognized and respected. This is the promise of Kalkiism—a new world order rooted in shared humanity and collective progress.

Call to Action

The journey toward a Kalkiist world begins with imagination and action. It requires individuals, communities, and nations to challenge the status quo and embrace a vision of fairness and inclusion.

To realize this future, we must:

- **Educate Ourselves**: Understand the principles of Kalkiism and how they address global challenges.
- **Advocate for Change**: Share the vision of Kalkiism with others, building momentum for its adoption.
- **Participate in Pilots**: Support local initiatives that test Kalkiist principles and demonstrate their benefits.
- **Collaborate Globally**: Engage with international efforts to promote equity, sustainability, and peace.

Kalkiism is not just an economic framework; it is a call to reimagine what is possible. Together, we can create a world where resources are shared, opportunities are equal, and progress benefits everyone. The future is ours to shape—let us choose a path of cooperation, dignity, and hope.

Conclusion: The Promise of Kalkiism

Throughout history, humanity has continually sought to create systems that reflect its highest ideals—justice, equality, and prosperity. Economic paradigms such as capitalism and communism have shaped the modern world, each bringing successes and failures. Yet, neither system has managed to eradicate poverty, eliminate inequality, or ensure a sustainable future. Kalkiism, a revolutionary framework, offers a new path forward. By replacing traditional currency with time as the universal measure of value and prioritizing Gross Domestic Requirement (GDR) over Gross Domestic Product (GDP), Kalkiism redefines how societies function, fostering fairness, inclusivity, and abundance.

Kalkiism is not communism. While both systems aim to address inequality, Kalkiism avoids the pitfalls of centralized control and inefficiency that have historically plagued communist regimes. Nor is it capitalism, which prioritizes profit over people and perpetuates economic hierarchies. Instead, Kalkiism is a fundamentally new approach that combines the best elements of innovation, equity, and sustainability. It balances individual freedom with collective responsibility, ensuring that every person's contributions are valued equally, and every individual's needs are met.

At the heart of Kalkiism lies a profound respect for human dignity. By valuing all labor equally, whether it is caregiving, teaching, or engineering, Kalkiism acknowledges the intrinsic worth of every individual. Its time-based economy eliminates the inequalities fostered by monetary wealth, ensuring that no one is excluded from participating in or benefiting from the economy. This redefinition of value has the power to transform societies, replacing competition with cooperation and scarcity with abundance.

The transformative potential of Kalkiism extends beyond individual communities. On a global scale, it offers solutions to pressing challenges such as poverty, climate change, and geopolitical tensions. By aligning economic activity with human needs and environmental sustainability, Kalkiism fosters international cooperation and solidarity. It envisions a world where resources are shared equitably, innovation benefits all, and nations collaborate for the common good.

Critics may dismiss Kalkiism as utopian, but its principles are grounded in practicality and scalability. Technological advancements, such as blockchain for transparent transactions and AI for resource optimization, make its implementation increasingly feasible. Moreover, Kalkiism does not demand an immediate overhaul of existing systems. Instead, it advocates for incremental change, starting with pilot programs and local initiatives that demonstrate its benefits and build public trust.

The promise of Kalkiism is not just economic—it is deeply human. It challenges us to reimagine what is possible and to build a future where fairness and opportunity are universal. It is a call to action, inviting individuals, communities, and nations to embrace a vision of equity and sustainability.

As we face the challenges of the 21st century, from rising inequality to environmental crises, Kalkiism offers a beacon of hope. It is a reminder that humanity has the power to innovate, adapt, and create systems that reflect our highest aspirations. Kalkiism is more than an economic paradigm—it is a promise of a better world.

Epilogue: From Theory to Practice – The Path to Implementing Kalkiism in Nepal

The intellectual discourse around Kalkiism, with its revolutionary approach to economics and society, has reached a pivotal juncture. While the debates on its principles and comparisons to existing systems like capitalism and communism have been enlightening, the time has come to move beyond abstract theory. The next step is the pragmatic application of Kalkiism in a real-world setting, and the chosen pilot project country is Nepal. A nation with rich cultural heritage, diverse communities, and a history of political evolution, Nepal presents a unique opportunity to pioneer the Kalkiist economy.

For this vision to materialize, several interconnected steps are required. These include organizing a robust political campaign to ensure that the newly formed political entity, the **Satyug Samaj Party**, gains widespread support and electoral success in Nepal. Additionally, the transition to a Kalkiist economy must be meticulously planned to ensure minimal disruption to people's lives, reassuring citizens that their current living standards and properties, like the houses they inhabit, will remain secure. This essay explores the roadmap to turning Kalkiism from an intellectual ideal into a practical reality in Nepal.

Nepal as the Chosen Pilot Project

Nepal, a landlocked country nestled in the Himalayas, is uniquely suited to become the testing ground for Kalkiism. Its socio-political and economic conditions present a compelling case for pioneering this revolutionary system.

1. A Nation Ready for Change

Nepal has undergone significant political changes in recent decades, transitioning from a monarchy to a federal democratic republic. While democracy has brought some progress, systemic issues like poverty, unemployment, and inequality persist.

- **Poverty and Inequality**: Despite advancements, approximately 17% of the population lives below the poverty

line. The economic disparity between urban and rural areas remains stark.
- **Unemployment**: Many Nepalese youth migrate abroad for work, leaving the domestic labor market underutilized.

These challenges make Nepal fertile ground for introducing Kalkiism, which promises to address inequality, provide universal access to basic needs, and create vibrant local economies.

2. A Tradition of Community and Cooperation

Nepalese society is deeply rooted in community-oriented values, making it more receptive to Kalkiism's cooperative ethos. From traditional farming cooperatives to communal rituals and celebrations, the culture already embodies the spirit of collaboration that Kalkiism seeks to amplify.

3. Manageable Scale for Implementation

With a population of approximately 30 million, Nepal is large enough to showcase Kalkiism's viability but small enough to manage the complexities of a systemic overhaul. Its size makes it an ideal pilot project before scaling Kalkiism to other nations.

The Satyug Samaj Party: A Political Vehicle for Change

For Kalkiism to become a reality in Nepal, it must be anchored within the political framework. The **Satyug Samaj Party** has been conceived as the political arm of this vision, tasked with winning elections and securing a mandate to implement Kalkiism.

1. Crafting a Compelling Political Narrative

The success of the Satyug Samaj Party depends on its ability to present Kalkiism as a transformative yet practical solution to Nepal's challenges. Key elements of this narrative include:

- **Addressing Economic Inequality**: Highlighting how Kalkiism will provide universal access to food, housing,

education, and healthcare through the Gross Domestic Requirement (GDR).
- **Job Creation and Retention**: Emphasizing how the time-based economy will create jobs across all sectors, including those undervalued in traditional GDP models, such as caregiving and household management.
- **Environmental Sustainability**: Showcasing Kalkiism's commitment to renewable energy, sustainable farming, and conservation—issues critical to Nepal's ecologically sensitive regions.

2. Building a Grassroots Movement

A political revolution requires mass mobilization. The Satyug Samaj Party must:

- **Engage Local Communities**: Through village meetings, town halls, and community events, party leaders must connect with citizens at the grassroots level.
- **Recruit Influential Advocates**: Gaining the support of respected community leaders, educators, and youth influencers can amplify the party's message.
- **Leverage Technology**: Social media platforms can be used to disseminate information about Kalkiism, debunk misconceptions, and mobilize younger voters.

3. Policy Priorities and Electoral Manifesto

The party's manifesto must provide clear and actionable steps for transitioning to a Kalkiist economy. Key policy proposals include:

- **Establishing GDR Metrics**: Introducing legislation to replace GDP with GDR as the primary measure of economic success.
- **Implementing Time-Based Wages**: Gradually transitioning sectors to the time-based economy, starting with pilot programs in select industries.
- **Securing Basic Needs**: Guaranteeing universal access to essential services like healthcare, education, and clean energy.

Ensuring a Smooth Transition

The transition from Nepal's current economic system to a Kalkiist economy must be carefully managed to avoid disruptions and build public trust.

1. Reassuring Citizens About Property Rights

One of the most significant concerns during such a transition is property ownership. Kalkiism must reassure citizens that:

- **You Get to Keep Your Home**: The houses people currently inhabit will remain theirs, ensuring stability and security.
- **Gradual Implementation**: Changes to the economy will be phased in over time, allowing citizens to adapt without fear of losing their assets or livelihood.

2. Pilot Projects to Build Confidence

Before implementing Kalkiism nationwide, pilot programs can demonstrate its effectiveness. Examples include:

- **Time-Based Wages in Agriculture**: Introducing time-based compensation in farming cooperatives to showcase fairness and efficiency.
- **Healthcare Access**: Piloting universal healthcare in select districts, funded through time credits.
- **Community Markets**: Establishing local markets where goods and services are priced in time units, promoting equitable trade.

3. Leveraging Technology for Transparency

Technological tools can ensure that the transition is transparent and accountable.

- **Blockchain**: To manage time-credit transactions securely and transparently.
- **AI-Driven Resource Allocation**: To optimize the distribution of resources based on GDR metrics.

Challenges and Solutions

Transitioning to a Kalkiist economy in Nepal will inevitably face challenges. Addressing these proactively is crucial for success.

1. Resistance from Established Interests

Wealthy elites and businesses benefiting from the current system may resist Kalkiism.

- **Solution**: Engage in dialogue to demonstrate how Kalkiism benefits all by reducing societal instability and fostering a cooperative economy.

2. Public Skepticism

Many may view Kalkiism as too radical or idealistic.

- **Solution**: Provide tangible examples of Kalkiism's success through pilot projects and communicate its principles clearly and repeatedly.

3. Resource Constraints

Implementing systemic change requires significant resources.

- **Solution**: Partner with international organizations and seek technical and financial support from allies interested in testing innovative economic models.

The Global Implications of Nepal's Experiment

If successfully implemented in Nepal, Kalkiism could serve as a blueprint for other nations facing similar challenges.

- **Inspiring Neighboring Countries**: Nepal's success could inspire South Asian neighbors, like India and Bangladesh, to consider adopting elements of Kalkiism.

- **A Model for the Global South**: Developing nations worldwide could look to Nepal as an example of how to align economic systems with human and environmental well-being.

A Call to Action

The intellectual debate around Kalkiism has laid a solid foundation, but the real challenge lies in its implementation. Nepal's journey to becoming the first Kalkiist nation requires collective effort, strategic planning, and unwavering commitment.

- **For Nepal's Citizens**: This is an opportunity to embrace a system that promises fairness, dignity, and prosperity for all.
- **For the Global Community**: Supporting Nepal in this endeavor could pave the way for a new era of economic justice and sustainability.

Kalkiism is not just an economic model; it is a vision for a better world. Nepal's experiment is the first step toward turning that vision into reality. With the right leadership, collaboration, and determination, the transition to Kalkiism can usher in a new age of equality and abundance—not just for Nepal, but for humanity as a whole.

www.ingramcontent.com/pod-product-compliance
Lightning Source LLC
Chambersburg PA
CBHW082253220526
45469CB00009B/2991